tapas

This is a Parragon Publishing Book
This edition published in 2006

Parragon Publishing
Queen Street House
4 Queen Street
Bath BA1 1HE, UK

Copyright © Parragon Books Ltd 2004

All rights reserved. No part of this publication may be
reproduced, stored in a retrieval system, or transmitted, in any
form or by any means, electronic, mechanical, photocopying,
recording, or otherwise, without the prior permission of the
copyright holder.

ISBN: 1-40548-317-2

Printed in China

Produced by the Bridgewater Book Company Ltd.
Project Designer: Michael Whitehead
Project Editor: Anna Samuels
Photographer: David Jordan
Home Economist: Jacqueline Bellefontaine
Cover design by Phily McIvor

Notes for the Reader
This book uses imperial, metric, or US cup measurements. Follow
the same units of measurement throughout; do not mix imperial
and metric. All spoon measurements are level: teaspoons are
assumed to be 5 ml, and tablespoons are assumed to be 15 ml.
Unless otherwise stated, milk is assumed to be whole, eggs and
individual vegetables such as potatoes are medium, and pepper
is freshly ground black pepper.

Recipes using raw or very lightly cooked eggs should be avoided by
infants, the elderly, pregnant women, convalescents, and anyone
suffering from an illness. Pregnant and breastfeeding women are
also advised to avoid eating peanuts and peanut products.

contents

introduction

TAPAS dishes are quick and easy to prepare and can be served both hot and cold. Hopping from bar to bar tasting different tapas dishes is part of Spanish life. Tapas are also ideal dishes for serving on special occasions.

Tapas, which originated in Spain, are appetizers that can be served either hot or cold. They are normally served with chilled white wine, beer, or sherry and can be found in most bars and wine bars (*tascas* and *bodegas*) all over Spain.

They are normally served before lunch and dinner. Tapas are so versatile that they can also be prepared and eaten on special occasions and at parties, either served at the table or presented as part of a buffet selection.

Tapas were invented in Andalusia, a wine-making region in southern Spain. The word tapas comes via the Spanish verb tapar, which means "to cover," and tapa is the word for "a lid." In this region a piece of bread would be placed over a person's wine glass in order to keep the flies and dust away.

The Andalusians then gradually thought of placing other items of food on top of the bread and this is how tapas originated.

It is best to serve the tapas dishes in small earthenware bowls, as these are good for keeping the food warm or cold. However, if you do not

The Cheese & Eggs section is equally varied and includes recipes that use Parmesan, Manchego, and Cheddar cheese. The Cheese Puffs with Fiery Tomato Salsa is clearly a dish for those who like hot food! If you are able to find Manchego cheese, then the Fried Manchego Cheese dish is an excellent tapa to have with chilled wine.

Finally, the Fish & Seafood section includes a huge variety of recipes, a reflection of the choice of fish that is on offer in Spain! The Sardines Marinated in Sherry Vinegar are delicious and the same recipe can be made with fresh trout or salmon fillets.

It is a good idea to have toothpicks available for the tapas and a small dish or saucer for the discarded toothpicks.

have small bowls, ordinary serving dishes will also be fine.

Included in this book is a fine selection of tasty recipes that truly represent traditional food associated with Spain. The number and diversity of tapas that exist are amazing. This book is divided into four parts: Meat & Poultry, Vegetables, Cheese & Eggs, Fish & Seafood.

The Meat & Poultry section includes a wide selection of recipes which draw on chorizo, the popular sausage, chicken, serrano ham, and pork.

The Vegetables section is colorful and draws on a range of vegetables, such as green beans, eggplants, potatoes, tomatoes, and spinach. The Salted Almonds recipe is very popular and really versatile, as walnut halves, pistachios, peanuts, and cashews can also be used.

meat & poultry

INCLUDED in this section are eleven tasty meat and poultry recipes. The chorizo sausage recipes are popular and are very quick and easy to prepare. There are also other equally tasty dishes using chicken, ham, and pork.

garlic fried bread & chorizo

Choose a soft chorizo sausage for this recipe. Although it will not have been cured for a long period, the soft varieties usually contain a high proportion of fat, which makes them very good for cooking. As an alternative to chorizo, you could use thickly cut serrano ham or even garlic sausage. *SERVES 6–8 AS PART OF A TAPAS MEAL*

7 oz/200 g chorizo sausage, outer casing removed
4 thick slices 2-day-old country bread
Spanish olive oil, for shallow-frying
3 garlic cloves, finely chopped
2 tbsp chopped fresh flatleaf parsley
paprika, to garnish

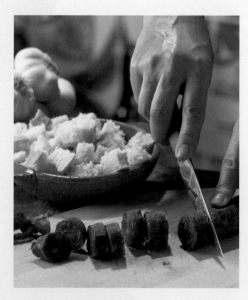

Cut the chorizo sausage into $^1/_2$-inch/1-cm thick slices and cut the bread, with its crusts still on, into $^1/_2$-inch/1-cm cubes. Add sufficient olive oil to a large, heavy-bottom skillet so that it generously covers the base. Heat the oil, then add the garlic and cook for 30 seconds–1 minute, or until lightly browned.

Add the bread cubes to the skillet and cook, stirring all the time, until golden brown and crisp. Add the chorizo slices and cook for 1–2 minutes, or until hot. Using a slotted spoon, remove the bread cubes and chorizo from the pan and drain well on paper towels.

Turn the fried bread and chorizo into a warmed serving bowl, then add the chopped parsley and toss them together. Garnish the dish with a sprinkling of paprika and serve warm. Accompany with toothpicks so that a piece of sausage and a cube of bread can be speared together for eating.

MEAT & POULTRY **11**

variation

If you are unable to find fresh artichokes, you could use 14 oz/400 g canned artichoke hearts. Drain the juices and slice the artichoke hearts in half. As a variation, you could use serrano ham, cut in one thick piece rather than sliced, instead of the chorizo.

melon, chorizo & artichoke salad

Chorizo is so versatile and can be combined with fruit and vegetables.

SERVES 8 AS PART OF A TAPAS MEAL

12 small globe artichokes

juice of 1/2 lemon

2 tbsp Spanish olive oil

1 small orange-fleshed melon,

such as cantaloupe

7 oz/200 g chorizo sausage,

outer casing removed

few sprigs of fresh tarragon or

flatleaf parsley, to garnish

dressing

3 tbsp Spanish extra virgin olive oil

1 tbsp red wine vinegar

1 tsp prepared mustard

1 tbsp chopped fresh tarragon

salt and pepper

To prepare the artichokes, cut off the stems. With your hands, break off the toughest outer leaves at the base until the tender inside leaves are visible. Using a pair of scissors, cut the spiky tips off the leaves. Using a sharp knife, pare the dark green skin from the base and down the stem. As you prepare the artichokes, brush the cut surfaces with lemon juice to prevent discoloration. Alternatively, you could fill a bowl with cold water to which you have added a little lemon juice, and immerse the artichokes in the acidulated water to prevent the discoloration. Carefully remove the choke (the mass of silky hairs) by pulling it out with your fingers or by scooping it out with a spoon. It is very important to remove all of the choke, as the little barbs, if eaten, can irritate the throat. However, if you are using very young artichokes, you do not need to worry about removing the choke and you can include the stem too, well scraped, as it will be quite tender. Cut the artichokes into fourths and brush them again with lemon juice.

Heat the olive oil in a large, heavy-bottom skillet, then add the prepared artichokes and cook, stirring frequently, for 5 minutes. Remove from the skillet and transfer to a large bowl, then let cool.

To prepare the melon, cut in half and scoop out the seeds with a spoon. Cut the flesh into bite-size cubes. Add to the cooled artichokes. Cut the chorizo into bite-size chunks and add to the melon and artichokes.

To make the dressing, put all the ingredients in a small bowl and whisk together. Just before serving, pour the dressing over the prepared salad ingredients and toss together. Serve the salad garnished with tarragon sprigs.

chorizo in red wine

It is also fun to make this dish with small, individual chorizo sausages. Prepare them in exactly the same way but, after removing their outer casing, keep them whole rather than slicing. *SERVES 6 AS PART OF A TAPAS MEAL*

7 oz/200 g chorizo sausage
generous ³/₄ cup Spanish red wine
2 tbsp brandy (optional)
fresh flatleaf parsley, to garnish
crusty bread, to serve

Before you begin, bear in mind that this dish is best if prepared the day before you are planning to serve it.

Using a fork, prick the chorizo sausage in 3 or 4 places. Put it in a large pan and pour in the wine. Bring the wine to a boil, then reduce the heat and simmer gently, covered, for 15–20 minutes. Transfer the chorizo and wine to a bowl or dish, then cover and let the sausage marinate in the wine for 8 hours or overnight.

The next day, remove the chorizo from the bowl or dish and reserve the wine for later. Remove the outer casing from the chorizo and cut the sausage into ¹/₄-inch/5-mm slices. Place the slices in a large, heavy-bottom skillet or flameproof serving dish.

If you are adding the brandy, pour it into a small pan and heat gently. Pour the brandy over the chorizo slices, then stand well back and set alight. When the flames have died down, shake the pan gently, then add the reserved wine to the pan and cook over high heat until almost all of the wine has evaporated.

Serve the chorizo in red wine piping hot, in the dish in which it was cooked, with parsley to garnish. Accompany with chunks or slices of bread to mop up the juices and provide toothpicks to spear the pieces of chorizo.

variation

You can also use cider in place of
the red wine, since it is often used
in the north of Spain.

chorizo empanadillas

A tapas meal would not be complete without the inclusion of chorizo. In this recipe, it is encased in puff pastry and makes a delicious accompaniment to a glass of chilled white wine. *MAKES 12*

4¹/₂ oz/125 g chorizo sausage, outer casing removed
all-purpose flour, for dusting
9 oz/250 g ready-made puff pastry, thawed if frozen
beaten egg, to glaze
paprika and fresh basil, to garnish

Preheat the oven to 400°F/200°C. Cut the chorizo sausage into small dice measuring about ¹/₂ inch/ 1 cm square.

On a lightly floured counter, thinly roll out the puff pastry. Using a plain, round

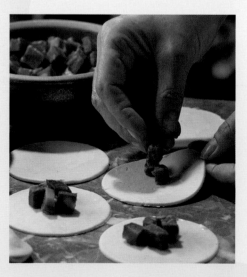

3¹/₄-inch/8-cm cutter, cut into circles. Gently pile the trimmings together and roll out again, then cut out additional circles to produce 12 in total. Put about 1 teaspoon of the chopped chorizo onto each of the pastry circles.

Dampen the edges of the pastry with a little water, then fold one half over the other half to cover the chorizo completely. Seal the edges together with your fingers. Using the prongs of a fork, press against the edges to give a decorative finish and seal them further. With the tip of a sharp knife, make a small slit in the side of each pastry. You can store the pastries in the refrigerator at this stage until you are ready to bake them.

Place the pastries onto dampened baking sheets and brush each with a little beaten egg to glaze. Bake in the oven for 10–15 minutes, or until golden brown and puffed. Using a small sifter, lightly dust the top of each empanadilla with a little paprika. Garnish with basil and serve the chorizo empanadillas hot or warm.

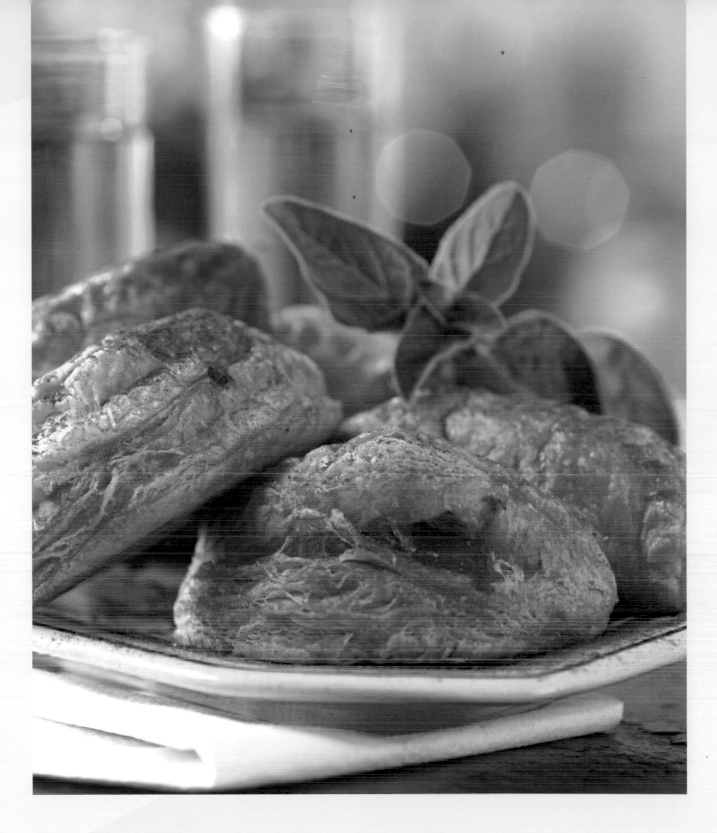

The empanadillas are particularly easy to prepare—in fact, something a child might like to make. Just watch that they don't eat all the chorizo before it reaches the oven!

MEAT & POULTRY   **17**

chicken in lemon & garlic

There are several variations to this popular, quick and easy-to-prepare tapa dish. Try, for example, using chicken wings or, in place of the chicken, use slices of fresh rabbit, turkey, or pork. *SERVES 6–8 AS PART OF A TAPAS MEAL*

4 large skinless, boneless chicken breasts

5 tbsp Spanish olive oil

1 onion, finely chopped

6 garlic cloves, finely chopped

grated rind of 1 lemon, finely pared rind of 1 lemon and juice of both lemons

4 tbsp chopped fresh flatleaf parsley, plus extra to garnish

salt and pepper

lemon wedges and crusty bread, to serve

Using a sharp knife, slice the chicken breasts widthwise into very thin slices. Heat the olive oil in a large, heavy-bottom skillet, then add the onion and cook for 5 minutes, or until softened but not browned. Add the garlic and cook for an additional 30 seconds.

Add the sliced chicken to the skillet and cook gently for 5–10 minutes, stirring from time to time, until all the ingredients are lightly browned and the chicken is tender.

Add the grated lemon rind and lemon juice and let it bubble. At the same time, deglaze the skillet by scraping and stirring all the bits on the bottom of the skillet into the juices with a wooden spoon. Remove the skillet from the heat, then stir in the parsley and season to taste with salt and pepper.

Transfer the chicken in lemon and garlic, piping hot, to a warmed serving dish. Sprinkle with the pared lemon rind and garnish with the parsley. Serve with lemon wedges for squeezing over the chicken, accompanied by chunks or slices of crusty bread for mopping up the lemon and garlic juices.

crispy chicken & ham croquettes

These cylindrical croquettes are very popular and served throughout Spain.

MAKES 8

4 tbsp olive oil or $^1/_2$ stick butter

4 tbsp all-purpose flour

generous $^3/_4$ cup milk

4 oz/115 g cooked chicken, ground

2 oz/55 g serrano or cooked ham, very finely chopped

1 tbsp chopped fresh flatleaf parsley, plus extra sprigs to garnish

small pinch of freshly grated nutmeg

salt and pepper

1 egg, beaten

1 cup day-old white bread crumbs

corn oil, for deep-frying

Aïoli (see page 53), to serve

Heat the olive oil in a pan. Stir in the flour to form a paste and cook gently, stirring, for 1 minute. Remove the pan from the heat and stir in the milk until smooth. Return to the heat and slowly bring to a boil, stirring all the time, until the mixture boils and thickens.

Remove the pan from the heat, then add the ground chicken and beat until the mixture is smooth. Add the chopped ham, parsley, and nutmeg and mix well together. Season the mixture to taste with salt and pepper. Spread the chicken mixture in a dish and let stand for 30 minutes, or until cool, then cover and put in the refrigerator for 2–3 hours or overnight. Do not be tempted to miss out this stage, as chilling the croquettes helps to stop them falling apart when they are cooked.

When the chicken mixture has chilled, pour the beaten egg onto a plate and spread the bread crumbs out on a separate plate. Divide the chicken mixture into 8 equal-size portions. With dampened hands, form each portion into a cylindrical shape. Dip the croquettes, one at a time, in the beaten egg, then roll in the bread crumbs to coat them. Place on a plate and chill in the refrigerator for about 1 hour.

To cook the croquettes, heat the oil in a deep fryer to 350–375°F/180–190°C, or until a cube of bread browns in 30 seconds. Add the croquettes, in batches to prevent the temperature of the oil dropping, and cook for 5–10 minutes. Remove from the deep fryer with a slotted spoon and drain well on paper towels.

Serve the chicken and ham croquettes piping hot, garnished with parsley sprigs and accompanied by a bowl of aïoli for dipping.

cook's tip

These crispy croquettes are another very popular tapa served all over Spain and come in an enormous variety of flavors and in all shapes and sizes, from round and oval to flat and cylindrical.

You could add some halved or quartered
mushrooms and/or 1 tablespoon of drained
capers or chopped green olives.

chicken livers
in sherry sauce

This tapa dish is often served in Andalusia's tapas bars and is equally popular made with lamb's or calf's kidneys.

SERVES 6 AS PART OF A TAPAS MEAL

1 lb/450 g chicken livers	scant ¹/₂ cup dry Spanish sherry
2 tbsp Spanish olive oil	salt and pepper
1 small onion, finely chopped	2 tbsp chopped fresh flatleaf parsley
2 garlic cloves, finely chopped	crusty bread or toast, to serve

If necessary, trim the chicken livers, cutting away any ducts and gristle, then cut them into small, bite-size pieces.

Heat the olive oil in a large, heavy-bottom skillet. Add the onion and cook for 5 minutes, or until softened but not browned. Add the garlic and cook for an additional 30 seconds.

Add the chicken livers to the skillet and cook for 2–3 minutes, stirring all the time, until they are firm and have changed color on the outside but are still pink and soft in the center. Using a slotted spoon, lift the chicken livers from the skillet, then transfer them to a large, warmed serving dish or several smaller ones and keep warm.

Add the sherry to the skillet, then increase the heat and let it bubble for 3–4 minutes to evaporate the alcohol and reduce slightly. At the same time, deglaze the skillet by scraping and stirring all the bits on the bottom of the skillet into the sauce with a wooden spoon. Season the sauce to taste with salt and pepper.

Pour the sherry sauce over the chicken livers and sprinkle over the parsley. Serve piping hot, accompanied by chunks or slices of crusty bread or toast to mop up the sherry sauce.

fava beans with
serrano ham

Both fresh and dried fava beans are highly regarded in Spain.
In this recipe, you can use fresh or, if more convenient, frozen fava beans,
but if you choose the latter, make sure that they are baby ones, which are more tender.
If you have time, you can remove the skins from the beans to reveal
the soft, bright-green bean inside, but it is a time-consuming task!

SERVES 6–8 AS PART OF A TAPAS MEAL

**2 oz/55 g serrano ham, prosciutto, pancetta,
or rindless smoked lean bacon
4 oz/115 g chorizo sausage,
outer casing removed
4 tbsp Spanish olive oil
1 onion, finely chopped
2 garlic cloves, finely chopped
splash of dry white wine
1 lb/450 g frozen fava beans, thawed,
or about 3 lb/1.3 kg fresh fava beans in their
pods, shelled to give 1 lb/450 g
1 tbsp chopped fresh dill or mint,
plus extra sprigs to garnish
pinch of sugar
salt and pepper**

Using a sharp knife, cut the ham, prosciutto, pancetta, or bacon into small strips. Cut the chorizo into 3/4-inch/2-cm cubes. Heat the olive oil in a large, heavy-bottom skillet or flameproof dish that has a lid. Add the onion and cook for 5 minutes, or until softened and beginning to brown. If you are using pancetta or bacon, add it with the onion. Add the garlic and cook for an additional 30 seconds.

Pour the wine into the skillet, then increase the heat and let it bubble to evaporate the alcohol. Reduce the heat, then add the fava beans, ham, if using, and the chorizo and cook for 1–2 minutes, stirring all the time to coat in the oil.

Cover the skillet and let the beans simmer very gently in the oil, stirring from time to time, for 10–15 minutes, or until the beans are tender. It may be necessary to add a little water to the skillet during cooking, so keep an eye on it and add a splash if the beans become too dry. Stir in the dill and sugar. Season with salt and pepper, but taste first because it may not need any salt.

Transfer the fava beans to a large, warmed serving dish, several smaller ones, or individual plates, and serve piping hot, garnished with dill sprigs.

tiny spanish meatballs
in almond sauce

Ground pork, or a combination of pork and veal, is the most traditional meat used in Spain to make these meatballs, but there is no reason why you could not use ground lamb or beef, if preferred.

SERVES 6–8 AS PART OF A TAPAS MEAL

2 oz/55 g white or brown bread, crusts removed

3 tbsp water

4 cups fresh lean ground pork

1 large onion, finely chopped

1 garlic clove, crushed

2 tbsp chopped fresh flatleaf parsley, plus extra to garnish

1 egg, beaten

freshly grated nutmeg

salt and pepper

all-purpose flour, for coating

2 tbsp Spanish olive oil

squeeze of lemon juice

crusty bread, to serve

Almond Sauce

2 tbsp Spanish olive oil

1 oz/25 g white or brown bread

generous 3/4 cup blanched almonds

2 garlic cloves, finely chopped

2/3 cup dry white wine

salt and pepper

13/4 cups vegetable stock

To prepare the meatballs, put the bread in a bowl, then add the water and let soak for 5 minutes. With your hands, squeeze out the water and return the bread to the dried bowl. Add the pork, onion, garlic, parsley, and egg, then season generously with grated nutmeg and a little salt and pepper. Knead the ingredients well together to form a smooth mixture.

Spread some flour on a plate. With floured hands, shape the meat mixture into about 30 equal-size balls, then roll each meatball again in flour until coated.

Heat the olive oil in a large, heavy-bottom skillet. Add the meatballs, in batches so that they do not overcrowd the skillet, and cook for 4–5 minutes, or until browned on all sides. Using a slotted spoon, remove the meatballs from the skillet and set aside.

To make the almond sauce, heat the olive oil in the same skillet in which the meatballs were fried. Break the bread into pieces, then add to the skillet with the almonds and cook gently, stirring frequently, until the bread and almonds are golden brown. Add the garlic and cook for an additional

30 seconds, then pour in the wine and boil for 1–2 minutes. Season to taste with salt and pepper and let cool slightly.

Transfer the almond mixture to a food processor. Pour in the vegetable stock and blend the mixture until smooth. Return the almond sauce to the skillet.

Carefully add the meatballs to the almond sauce and simmer for 25 minutes, or until the meatballs are tender. Taste the sauce and season with salt and pepper if necessary.

Transfer the cooked meatballs and almond sauce to a warmed serving dish, then add a squeeze of lemon juice to taste and sprinkle with chopped parsley to garnish.

This dish is best served piping hot with chunks or slices of crusty bread for mopping up the almond sauce.

roasted asparagus with mountain ham

The most popular Spanish ham is serrano, which means mountain ham, because it is cured in the mountains. It is then aged from several months to several years. If you are unable to obtain it, you could use Italian prosciutto instead. *MAKES 12*

2 tbsp Spanish olive oil
6 slices serrano ham
12 asparagus spears
pepper
Aïoli (see page 53), to serve

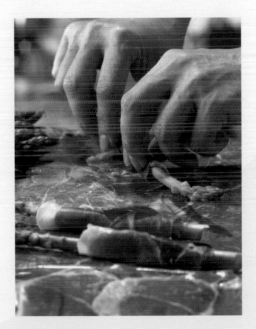

Preheat the oven to 400°F/200°C. Put half the olive oil in a roasting pan that will hold the asparagus spears in a single layer and swirl it around so that it covers the base. Cut each slice of serrano ham in half lengthwise.

Trim the ends of the asparagus spears, then wrap a slice of ham around the stem end of each spear. Place the wrapped spears in the prepared roasting pan and lightly brush the ham and asparagus with the remaining olive oil. Season the spears with pepper.

Roast the asparagus spears in the oven for about 10 minutes, depending on the thickness of the asparagus, until tender but still firm. Do not overcook the asparagus spears because it is important that they are still firm, so that you can pick them up with your fingers.

Serve the roasted asparagus with mountain ham piping hot, with a bowl of aïoli for dipping.

miniature pork brochettes

Although usually made with pork in Spain, these brochettes are of Arab origin
and would be made using lamb; both are delicious. *MAKES 12*

1 lb/450 g lean boneless pork
3 tbsp Spanish olive oil, plus extra
for oiling (optional)
grated rind and juice of
1 large lemon

2 garlic cloves, crushed
2 tbsp chopped fresh flatleaf parsley,
plus extra to garnish
1 tbsp ras-el-hanout spice blend
salt and pepper

The brochettes are marinated overnight, so remember to do this in advance, in order that they are ready when you need them. Cut the pork into pieces about 3/4 inch/2 cm square and put in a large, shallow, nonmetallic dish that will hold the pieces in a single layer.

To prepare the marinade, put all the remaining ingredients in a bowl and mix well together. Pour the marinade over the pork and toss the meat in it until well coated. Cover the dish and

let marinate in the refrigerator for 8 hours or overnight, stirring the pork 2–3 times.

You can use wooden or metal skewers to cook the brochettes, and for this recipe you will need about 12 x 6-inch/15-cm skewers. If you are using wooden ones, soak them in cold water for about 30 minutes prior to using. This helps to stop them burning and the food sticking to them during cooking. Metal skewers simply need to be greased, and flat ones should be used in preference to round ones to prevent the food on them falling off.

Preheat the broiler, grill pan, or grill. Thread about 3 marinated pork pieces, leaving a little space between each piece, onto each prepared skewer. Cook the brochettes for 10–15 minutes, or until tender and lightly charred, turning several times and basting with the remaining marinade during cooking. Serve the pork brochettes piping hot, garnished with parsley.

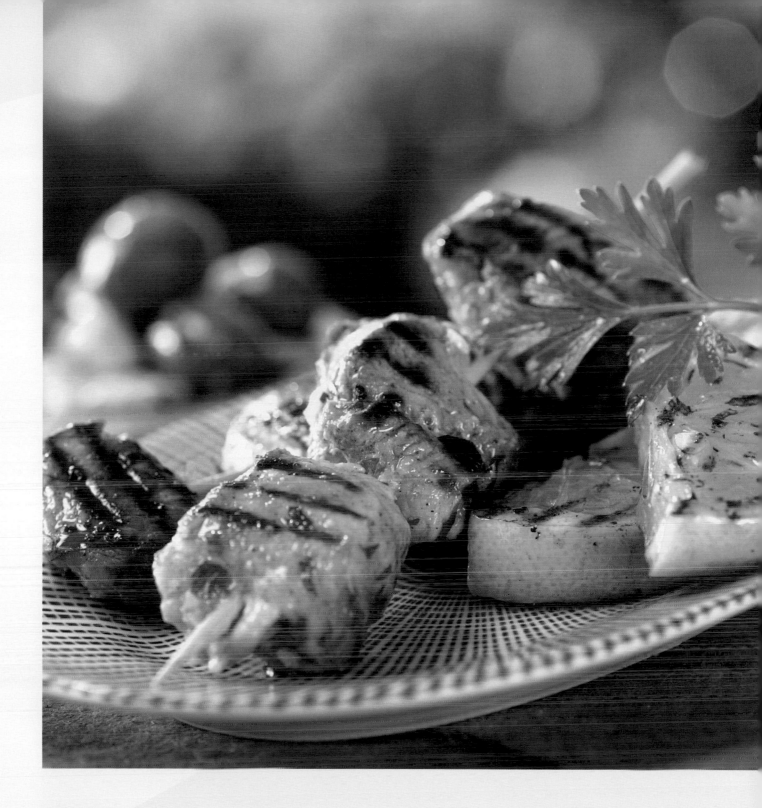

cook's tip

The ras-el-hanout spice blend consists
of galangal, rosebuds, black peppercorns,
ginger, cardamom, nigella, cayenne, allspice,
lavender, cinnamon, cassia, coriander, mace,
nutmeg, and cloves!

vegetables

THE tapas dishes presented here are delicious and very colorful. From Stuffed Cherry Tomatoes and Roasted Bell Pepper Salad to Spanish Spinach & Tomato Pizzas, every recipe offers a selection of mouthwatering morsels.

cracked marinated olives

The olives will keep in the refrigerator for several months. In fact, the longer
you marinate them, the more their flavor will be enhanced. Use the oil in which
they have been marinated for cooking or in a salad dressing.
It will impart a delicious flavor to a dish. *SERVES 8 AS PART OF A TAPAS MEAL*

**1 lb/450 g can or jar unpitted large green
olives, drained
4 garlic cloves, peeled
2 tsp coriander seeds
1 small lemon
4 sprigs of fresh thyme
4 feathery stalks of fennel
2 small fresh red chilies (optional)
pepper
Spanish extra virgin olive oil, to cover**

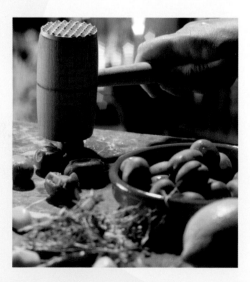

To allow the flavors of the marinade to penetrate the olives, place on a cutting board and, using a rolling pin, bash them lightly so that they crack slightly. Alternatively, use a sharp knife to cut a lengthwise slit in each olive as far as the stone. Using the flat side of a broad knife, lightly crush each garlic clove. Using a pestle and mortar, crack the coriander seeds. Cut the lemon, with its rind, into small chunks.

Put the olives, garlic, coriander seeds, lemon chunks, thyme sprigs, fennel, and chilies, if using, in a large bowl and toss together. Season with pepper to taste, but you should not need to add salt since conserved olives are usually salty enough. Pack the ingredients tightly into a glass jar with a lid. Pour in enough olive oil to cover the olives, then seal the jar tightly.

Let the olives stand at room temperature for 24 hours, then marinate in the refrigerator for at least 1 week, preferably 2 weeks. From time to time, gently give the jar a shake to re-mix the ingredients. Return the olives to room temperature and remove from the oil to serve. Provide toothpicks for spearing the olives.

salted almonds

Almonds are the most popular nut to be salted and served as a tapa in Spain,
but hazelnuts are also popular and can be prepared in exactly the same way.
Walnut halves, pistachios, peanuts, and cashews could also be given the same treatment.

SERVES 6–8 AS PART OF A TAPAS MEAL

**generous 1¹/₂ cups whole almonds, in their
skins or blanched (see method)
4 tbsp Spanish olive oil
coarse sea salt
1 tsp paprika or ground cumin (optional)**

Preheat the oven to 350°F/180°C. Fresh almonds in their skins are superior in taste, but blanched almonds are much more convenient. If the almonds are not blanched, put them in a bowl and cover with boiling water for 3–4 minutes, then plunge them into cold water for 1 minute. Drain them well in a strainer, then slide off the skins between your fingers. Dry the almonds well on paper towels.

Put the olive oil in a roasting pan and swirl it around so that it covers the base. Add the almonds and toss them in the pan so that they are evenly coated in the oil, then spread them out in a single layer.

Roast the whole almonds in the oven for 20 minutes, or until they are light golden brown, tossing several times during the cooking. Drain the almonds on paper towels, then transfer them to a bowl.

While the almonds are still warm, sprinkle with plenty of sea salt and the paprika, if using, and toss well together to coat. Serve warm or cold. The almonds are at their best when served freshly cooked, so, if possible, cook them on the day that you plan to eat them. However, they can be stored in an airtight container for up to 3 days.

sautéed garlic mushrooms

Exotic mushrooms such as boletuses or chanterelles can be used in place of cultivated mushrooms. *SERVES 6 AS PART OF A TAPAS MEAL*

1 lb/450 g white mushrooms
5 tbsp Spanish olive oil
2 garlic cloves, finely chopped
squeeze of lemon juice
salt and pepper
4 tbsp chopped fresh
flatleaf parsley
crusty bread, to serve

Wipe or brush clean the mushrooms, then trim off the stems close to the caps. Cut the large mushrooms in half or into fourths. Heat the olive oil in a large, heavy-bottom skillet, then add the garlic and cook for 30 seconds–1 minute, or until lightly browned.

Add the mushrooms and sauté over high heat, stirring most of the time, until they have absorbed all of the oil in the skillet.

Reduce the heat to low. When the juices have come out of the mushrooms, increase the heat again and sauté for 4–5 minutes, stirring most of the time, until the juices have almost evaporated. Add a squeeze of lemon juice and season to taste with salt and pepper. Stir in the parsley and cook for an additional 1 minute.

Transfer the sautéed mushrooms to a warmed serving dish and serve piping hot or warm. Accompany with chunks or slices of crusty bread for mopping up the garlic cooking juices.

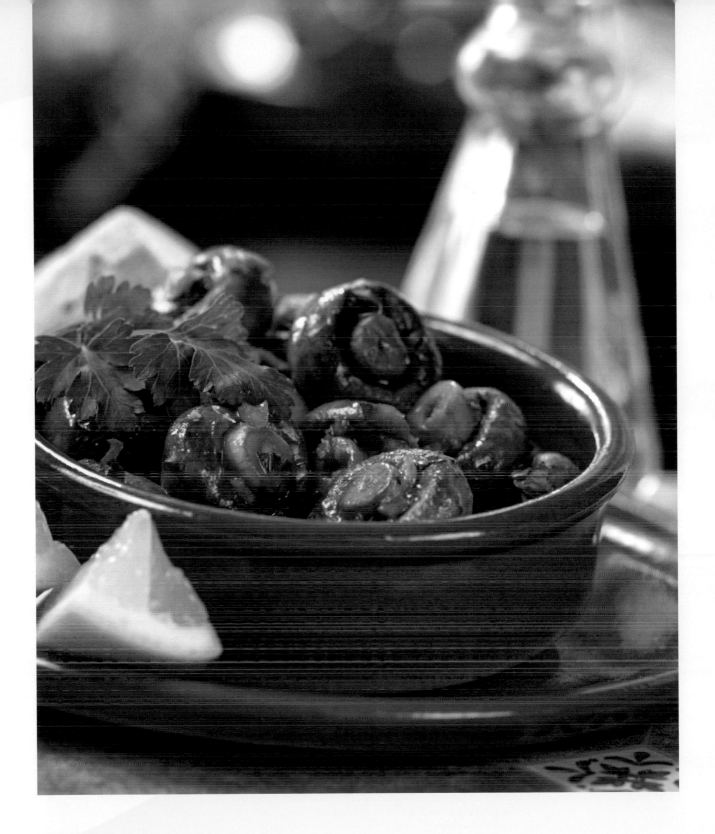

variation

Zucchini may also be prepared in the same
way, with a finely chopped small onion
cooked in the oil until lightly browned before
adding the garlic.

stuffed cherry tomatoes

Cherry tomatoes are made for just one mouthful but, if you prefer,

larger tomatoes could be stuffed with the fillings.

The quantities given in the recipe will fill about 10 medium tomatoes.

SERVES 8 AS PART OF A TAPAS MEAL

24 cherry tomatoes

Anchovy & Olive Filling
1³/4 oz/50 g canned anchovy fillets in olive oil
8 pimiento-stuffed green olives, finely chopped
2 large hard-cooked eggs, finely chopped
pepper

OR

Crab Mayonnaise Filling
6 oz/175 g canned crabmeat, drained
4 tbsp mayonnaise
1 tbsp chopped fresh
flatleaf parsley
salt and pepper

OR

Black Olive & Caper Filling
12 pitted black olives
3 tbsp capers
6 tbsp Aïoli (see page 53)
salt and pepper

Several different choices of filling have been given in this recipe, so make a decision before you begin. Alternatively, of course, you could make a selection of each. Simply cut the filling quantities to stuff the corresponding number of tomatoes.

If necessary, cut and discard a very thin slice from the stem end of each tomato to make the bases flat and stable. Cut a thin slice from the smooth end of each tomato and reserve for lids. Using a serrated knife or teaspoon, loosen the pulp and seeds of each and scoop out, discarding the flesh. Turn the scooped-out tomatoes upside down on paper towels and let drain for 5 minutes.

To make the anchovy and olive filling, drain the anchovies, reserving the oil for later, then chop finely and put in a bowl. Add the olives and hard-cooked eggs. Pour in a trickle of oil from the drained anchovies to moisten the mixture, then season with pepper (do not add salt to season, as the anchovies are salted) and mix well together.

To make the crab mayonnaise filling, put the crabmeat, mayonnaise, and parsley in a bowl and mix well together. Season the filling to taste.

To make the black olive and caper filling, put the olives and capers on paper towels to drain them well, then chop finely and put in a bowl. Add the Aïoli and mix well together. Season the filling to taste with salt and pepper.

Fill a pastry bag fitted with a 3/4-inch/2-cm plain tip with the filling of your choice and use to pack the filling into the hollow tomato shells. Store the tomatoes in the refrigerator until ready to serve.

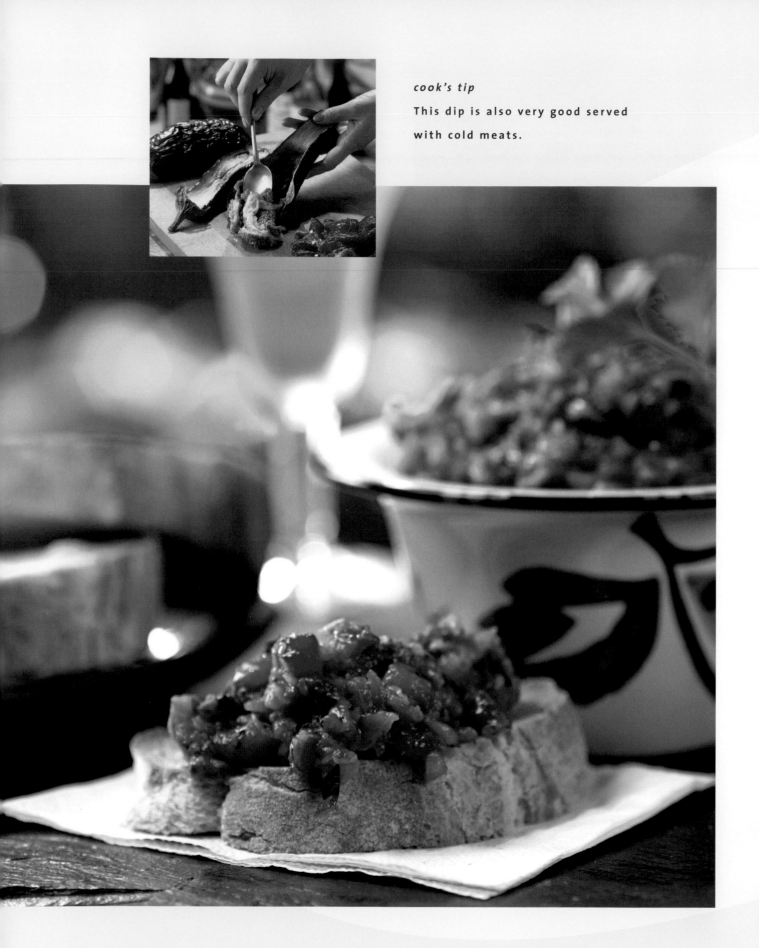

cook's tip
This dip is also very good served
with cold meats.

eggplant & bell pepper dip

Instead of cooking the eggplants and bell peppers in the oven,
they can be cooked under the broiler until the skins are charred all over.
They do, however, need to be turned frequently and they will
take about 10 minutes. *SERVES 6–8 AS PART OF A TAPAS MEAL*

Preheat the oven to 375°F/190°C. Prick the skins of the eggplants and bell peppers all over with a fork and brush with about 1 tablespoon of the olive oil. Put on a baking sheet and bake in the oven for 45 minutes, or until the skins are beginning to turn black, the flesh of the eggplant is very soft, and the bell peppers are deflated.

When the vegetables are cooked, put them in a bowl and immediately cover tightly with a clean, damp dish towel. Alternatively, you can put the vegetables in a plastic bag. Let them rest for about 15 minutes, or until they are cool enough to handle.

When the vegetables have cooled, cut the eggplants in half lengthwise, then carefully scoop out the flesh and discard the skin. Cut the eggplant flesh into large chunks. Remove and discard the stem, core, and seeds from the bell peppers and cut the flesh into large pieces.

Heat the remaining olive oil in a large, heavy-bottom skillet, then add the eggplant flesh and bell pepper pieces and cook for 5 minutes. Add the garlic and cook for an additional 30 seconds.

2 large eggplants

2 red bell peppers

4 tbsp Spanish olive oil

2 garlic cloves, coarsely chopped

grated rind and juice of 1/2 lemon

1 tbsp chopped cilantro,
**   plus extra sprigs to garnish**

1/2–1 tsp paprika

salt and pepper

bread or toast, to serve

Turn all the contents of the skillet onto paper towels to drain, then transfer to the bowl of a food processor. Add the lemon rind and juice, the chopped cilantro, the paprika, and salt and pepper according to taste, and blend until a speckled purée is formed.

Turn the eggplant and bell pepper dip into a serving bowl. Serve warm, at room temperature, or let cool for 30 minutes, then chill in the refrigerator for at least 1 hour and serve cold. Garnish with cilantro sprigs and accompany with thick slices of bread or toast for dipping.

stuffed pimientos

Make sure that you buy whole sweet peppers, not sliced. *MAKES 7–8*

There is a choice of fillings provided in this recipe —the final decision is yours. Lift the sweet peppers from the jar, reserving the oil for later.

To make the curd cheese and herb filling, put the curd cheese in a bowl and add the lemon juice, garlic, parsley, mint, and oregano. Mix well together. Season to taste with salt and pepper.

To make the tuna mayonnaise filling, put the tuna in a bowl and add the mayonnaise, lemon juice, and parsley. Add 1 tablespoon of the reserved oil from the jar of pimientos and mix well. Season to taste with salt and pepper.

To make the goat cheese and olive filling, put the olives in a bowl and add the goat cheese, garlic, and 1 tablespoon of the reserved oil from the jar of pimientos. Mix well together. Season to taste with salt and pepper.

Using a teaspoon, heap the filling of your choice into each pimiento. Put in the refrigerator and chill for at least 2 hours, or until firm.

To serve the pimientos, arrange them on a serving plate and, if necessary, wipe with paper towels to remove any of the filling that has spread over the skins. Garnish with herb sprigs.

6¹/₂ oz/185 g canned or bottled whole
   pimientos del piquillo
   (charbroiled sweet red peppers)
salt and pepper
fresh herb sprigs, to garnish

Curd Cheese & Herb Filling
8 oz/225 g curd cheese
1 tsp lemon juice
1 garlic clove, crushed
4 tbsp chopped fresh flatleaf parsley
1 tbsp chopped fresh mint
1 tbsp chopped fresh oregano
salt and pepper

OR
Tuna Mayonnaise Filling
7 oz/200 g canned tuna steak
   in olive oil, drained
5 tbsp mayonnaise
2 tsp lemon juice
2 tbsp chopped fresh flatleaf parsley
salt and pepper

OR

Goat Cheese & Olive Filling

scant ¹/₃ cup pitted black olives,
    finely chopped

7 oz/200 g soft goat cheese

1 garlic clove, crushed

salt and pepper

variation

Pimiento is simply the Spanish word for
pepper, but outside Spain the word is used to
refer to sweet red peppers that are cooked,
peeled, and sold in jars or cans. If you cannot
find pimientos del piquillo, look for a jar of
peppadew peppers from South Africa. This
recipe will fill about 36 peppadew peppers.

variation

Red and yellow bell peppers have been used
here, but there's no reason why you cannot
use green ones or a mixture.

roasted bell pepper salad

Although called roasted bell peppers, the bell peppers for this recipe are more usually broiled than roasted in an oven. You can also spear them on a fork and hold them over a gas flame, or roast them on a grill.

SERVES 8 AS PART OF A TAPAS MEAL

3 red bell peppers

3 yellow bell peppers

5 tbsp Spanish extra virgin olive oil

2 tbsp dry sherry vinegar or lemon juice

2 garlic cloves, crushed

pinch of sugar

salt and pepper

1 tbsp capers

8 small black Spanish olives

2 tbsp chopped fresh marjoram, plus extra sprigs to garnish

Preheat the broiler. Place the bell peppers on a wire rack or broiler pan and cook under a hot broiler for 10 minutes, or until the skins have blackened and blistered all over, turning them frequently.

Remove the roasted bell peppers from the heat, then put them in a bowl and immediately cover tightly with a clean, damp dish towel.

Alternatively, you can put the bell peppers in a plastic bag. You will find that the steam helps to soften the skins and makes it easier to remove them. Let the bell peppers stand for about 15 minutes, or until cool enough to handle.

Holding one bell pepper at a time over a bowl, use a knife to make a small hole in the base and squeeze out the juices, then reserve them. Still holding the bell pepper over the bowl, carefully peel off the blackened skin with your fingers or a knife and discard it. Cut the bell peppers in half and remove the stem, core, and seeds, then cut each bell pepper into neat thin strips. Arrange the bell pepper strips attractively on a serving dish.

To the reserved bell pepper juices add the olive oil, sherry vinegar, garlic, sugar, and salt and pepper to taste. Whisk together until combined. Drizzle the dressing evenly over the salad.

Scatter the capers, olives, and chopped marjoram over the salad. Garnish with marjoram sprigs. Serve at room temperature.

variation

This is one of Spain's most popular and staple tapas bar dishes. It varies, but the basic salad consists of potatoes, carrots, and peas, and sometimes tuna, as in this recipe.

russian salad

A very popular and colorful dish that can be stored in the refrigerator.

SERVES 8 AS PART OF A TAPAS MEAL

2 eggs

1 lb/450 g baby new potatoes,
cut into fourths

4 oz/115 g fine green beans, cut into
1-inch/2.5-cm lengths

4 oz/115 g frozen peas

4 oz/115 g carrots

7 oz/200 g canned tuna steak in olive oil, drained

2 tbsp lemon juice

8 tbsp mayonnaise

1 garlic clove, crushed

salt and pepper

4 small gherkins, sliced

8 pitted black olives, halved

1 tbsp capers

1 tbsp chopped fresh flatleaf parsley

1 tbsp chopped fresh dill, plus
extra sprigs to garnish

Put the eggs in a pan, then cover with cold water and slowly bring to a boil. Immediately reduce the heat to very low, then cover and simmer gently for 10 minutes. As soon as the eggs are cooked, drain them and put under cold running water until they are cold. By doing this quickly, you will prevent a black ring from forming around the egg yolk. Gently tap the eggs to crack the eggshells and let stand until cold.

Meanwhile, put the potatoes in a large pan of cold, salted water and bring to a boil. Reduce the heat and simmer for 7 minutes, or until tender. Add the beans and peas to the pan for the last 2 minutes of cooking. Drain well and splash under cold running water, then let the vegetables cool completely.

Cut the carrots into julienne strips about 1 inch/2.5 cm in length. Flake the tuna into large chunks. When the potatoes, beans, and peas are cold, put them in a large bowl. Add the carrot and the tuna and toss the ingredients together. Transfer the vegetables and tuna to a large dish.

In a pitcher, stir the lemon juice into the mayonnaise to thin it slightly. Stir in the garlic and season to taste with salt and pepper. Drizzle the mayonnaise dressing over the vegetables and tuna.

Scatter the gherkins, olives, and capers into the salad, then sprinkle over the parsley and dill. Store the salad in the refrigerator, but return to room temperature before serving. Peel the eggs and slice into wedges and add them to the salad, then garnish with dill sprigs.

fried potatoes
with piquant paprika

A variation is to cook the potatoes as here, then spoon over the Fiery Tomato Salsa that accompanies the Cheese Puffs (see page 62) or serve the salsa separately for dipping the potatoes in. This dish is then known as Patatas Bravas (Bold Potatoes). *SERVES 6 AS PART OF A TAPAS MEAL*

3 tsp paprika

1 tsp ground cumin

$^1/_4$–$^1/_2$ tsp cayenne pepper

$^1/_2$ tsp salt

1 lb/450 g small old potatoes, peeled

corn oil, for shallow-frying

Aïoli (see page 53), to serve (optional)

Put the paprika, cumin, the cayenne pepper, and salt in a small bowl and mix well together. Set aside.

Cut each potato into 8 thick wedges. Pour enough corn oil into a large, heavy-bottom skillet so that it comes about 1 inch/2.5 cm up the sides of the skillet. Heat the oil, then add the potato wedges, preferably in a single layer, and cook gently for 10 minutes, turning from time to time.

Remove from the skillet with a slotted spoon and drain on paper towels. Transfer the potato wedges to a large bowl and, while still hot, sprinkle them with the paprika mixture, then gently toss them together to coat.

Turn the fried potatoes with paprika into one large, warmed serving dish, several smaller ones, or individual plates and serve hot. Accompany with a bowl of aïoli for dipping, if wished.

baby potatoes with Aïoli

The recipe given here for Aïoli contains raw egg and therefore
should be avoided by infants, the elderly, pregnant women, convalescents,
and anyone suffering from an illness. If any of these cases applies to you,
use commercially made mayonnaise and add the crushed garlic to it.

SERVES 6–8 AS PART OF A TAPAS MEAL

1 lb/450 g baby new potatoes

**1 tbsp chopped fresh
flatleaf parsley**

salt

Aïoli

1 large egg yolk, at room temperature

1 tbsp white wine vinegar or lemon juice

2 large garlic cloves, peeled

salt and pepper

5 tbsp Spanish extra virgin olive oil

5 tbsp corn oil

To make the aïoli, put the egg yolk, vinegar, garlic, and salt and pepper to taste in a bowl and whisk until all ingredients blend well together. Add the olive, then the corn oil, drop by drop at first, and then, when it begins to thicken, in a slow, steady stream until the sauce is thick and smooth.

For this recipe, the Aïoli should be a little thin so that it coats the potatoes. To ensure this, quickly blend in 1 tablespoon water so that it forms the consistency of sauce.

To prepare the potatoes, cut them in half or fourths to make bite-size pieces. If they are very small, you can leave them whole. Put the potatoes in a large pan of cold, salted water and bring to a boil. Reduce the heat and simmer for 7 minutes, or until just tender. Drain well, then turn out into a large bowl.

While the potatoes are still warm, gently dip them in the Aïoli sauce. Dipping the potatoes in the sauce will help them to absorb the garlic flavor. Let the potatoes stand for about 20 minutes to marinate in the sauce.

Transfer the potatoes with Aïoli to a warmed serving dish, then sprinkle over the parsley and salt to taste and serve warm. Alternatively, the dish can be prepared ahead and stored in the refrigerator, but return it to room temperature before serving.

spanish spinach & tomato pizzas

One associates pizzas with Italy, but these Spanish pizzas are, in fact, very popular tapas dishes. They were traditionally made from a simple dough of flour and water, but now a bread or pastry base is used. The toppings can vary too and might include anchovies, bell peppers, ham, chorizo sausage, and olives, but seldom cheese. *MAKES 32*

2 tbsp Spanish olive oil, plus extra for brushing and drizzling

1 onion, finely chopped

1 garlic clove, finely chopped

14 oz/400 g canned chopped tomatoes

4¹/₂ oz/125 g baby spinach leaves

salt and pepper

scant ¹/₄ cup pine nuts

Bread Dough

4 tbsp warm water

¹/₂ tsp active dry yeast

pinch of sugar

1¹/₃ cups white bread flour, plus extra for dusting

¹/₂ tsp salt

To make the bread dough, measure the water into a small bowl, then sprinkle in the yeast and sugar and let stand in a warm place for 10–15 minutes, or until frothy.

Meanwhile, sift the flour and salt into a large bowl. Make a well in the center of the flour and pour in the yeast liquid, then mix together with a wooden spoon. Using your hands, work the mixture until it leaves the sides of the bowl clean.

Turn the dough out onto a lightly floured counter and knead for 10 minutes, or until smooth and elastic and no longer sticky. Shape into a ball and put it in a clean bowl. Cover with a clean, damp dish towel and let stand in a warm place for 1 hour, or until it has risen and doubled in size.

To make the topping, heat the olive oil in a large, heavy-bottom skillet. Add the onion and cook for 5 minutes, or until softened but not browned. Add the garlic and cook for an additional 30 seconds. Stir in the tomatoes and cook for 5 minutes, letting it bubble and stirring occasionally, until reduced to a thick mixture. Add the spinach leaves and cook, stirring, until they have wilted a little. Season the mixture to taste with salt and pepper.

While the dough is rising, preheat the oven to 400°F/200°C. Brush several baking sheets with olive oil. Turn the dough out onto a lightly floured counter and knead well for 2–3 minutes to knock out the air bubbles. Roll out the dough very, very thinly and, using a 2¹/₂-inch/6-cm plain, round cutter, cut out 32 circles. Place on the prepared baking sheets.

Spread each base with the spinach mixture to cover, then sprinkle the pine nuts over the top. Drizzle a little olive oil over each pizza. Bake in the oven for 10–15 minutes, or until the edges of the dough are golden brown. Serve the spinach and tomato pizzas hot.

zucchini fritters
with a dipping sauce

The exact same treatment can be applied to eggplants, while
the Pine Nut Sauce can be made with almonds in exactly the same
way too, if preferred. *SERVES 8 AS PART OF A TAPAS MEAL*

Whichever sauce you have chosen, make this first. To make the pine nut sauce, put the pine nuts and the garlic in a food processor and blend to form a purée. With the motor still running, gradually add the olive oil, lemon juice, and water to form a smooth sauce. Stir in the parsley and season to taste with salt and pepper. Turn into a serving bowl.

To prepare the zucchini, cut them on the diagonal into thin slices about 1/4 inch/5 mm thick. Put the flour and paprika in a plastic bag and mix together. Beat the egg and milk together in a large bowl.

Add the zucchini slices to the flour mixture and toss well together until coated. Shake off the excess flour. Heat the corn oil in a large, heavy-bottom skillet to a depth of about 1/2 inch/ 1 cm. Dip the zucchini slices, one at a time, into the egg mixture, then slip them into the hot oil. Cook the zucchini slices, in batches of a single layer, for 2 minutes, or until they are crisp and golden brown.

Using a slotted spoon, remove the zucchini fritters from the skillet and drain on paper towels.

1 lb/450 g baby zucchini

3 tbsp all-purpose flour

1 tsp paprika

1 large egg

2 tbsp milk

corn oil, for shallow-frying

coarse sea salt

dipping sauce such as Aïoli (see page 53),
    Fiery Tomato Salsa (see page 62)
        or Pine Nut Sauce (see below)

Pine Nut Sauce

scant 2/3 cup pine nuts

1 garlic clove, peeled

3 tbsp Spanish extra virgin olive oil

1 tbsp lemon juice

3 tbsp water

1 tbsp chopped fresh flatleaf parsley

salt and pepper

Continue until all the slices have been cooked. Serve the zucchini fritters piping hot, lightly sprinkled with sea salt. Accompany with a bowl of your chosen dipping sauce.

green beans
with pine nuts

As a variation to the pine nuts, you could use slivered or blanched almonds, which should be sliced into thin strips before cooking. They are equally delicious—it is simply a matter of personal preference. *SERVES 8 AS PART OF A TAPAS MEAL*

2 tbsp Spanish olive oil
¹/₃ cup pine nuts
¹/₂–1 tsp paprika
1 lb/450 g green beans
1 small onion, finely chopped
1 garlic clove, finely chopped
salt and pepper
juice of ¹/₂ lemon

Heat the oil in a large, heavy-bottom skillet, then add the pine nuts and cook for about 1 minute, stirring all the time and shaking the skillet, until light golden brown. Using a slotted spoon, remove the pine nuts from the skillet and drain well on paper towels, then transfer to a bowl. Reserve the oil in the skillet for later. Add the paprika, according to taste, to the pine nuts, and stir together until coated, then set aside.

If desired, trim the green beans and remove any strings. Put the beans in a pan and pour over boiling water, then return to a boil and cook for 5 minutes, or until tender but still firm. Drain well in a colander.

Reheat the oil in the skillet, then add the onion and cook for 5–10 minutes, or until softened and beginning to brown. Add the garlic and cook for an additional 30 seconds.

Add the beans to the skillet and cook for 2–3 minutes, tossing together with the onion until heated through. Season the beans to taste with salt and pepper.

Turn the contents of the skillet into a warmed serving dish, then sprinkle over the lemon juice and toss together. Scatter over the golden pine nuts and serve hot.

cheese & eggs

CHEESE and eggs are the basis of a wide range of tapas dishes. There are five recipes in this section, including the well-known Tortilla Española and dishes using a variety of cheeses, such as Manchego, Parmesan, and Cheddar.

cheese puffs
with fiery tomato salsa

These crisp little cheese puffs are light and fluffy. In this recipe they are served with a salsa, but they can, if preferred, simply be accompanied by small pickled cucumbers. Serve these speared on toothpicks so that a pickled cucumber and a cheese puff can be eaten together.

SERVES 8 AS PART OF A TAPAS MEAL

1/2 cup all-purpose flour

1/4 cup Spanish olive oil

2/3 cup water

2 eggs, beaten

2 oz/55 g Manchego, Parmesan, Cheddar, Gouda, or Gruyère cheese, finely grated

1/2 tsp paprika

salt and pepper

corn oil, for deep-frying

Fiery Tomato Salsa

2 tbsp Spanish olive oil

1 small onion, finely chopped

1 garlic clove, crushed

splash of dry white wine

14 oz/400 g canned chopped tomatoes

1 tbsp tomato paste

1/4–1/2 tsp red chili pepper flakes

dash of Tabasco sauce

pinch of sugar

salt and pepper

To make the salsa, heat the olive oil in a pan, then add the onion and cook for 5 minutes, or until softened but not browned. Add the garlic and cook for an additional 30 seconds. Add the wine and let bubble, then add all the remaining salsa ingredients to the pan and simmer, uncovered, for 10–15 minutes, or until a thick sauce is formed. Spoon into a serving bowl and set aside until ready to serve.

Meanwhile, prepare the cheese puffs. Sift the flour onto a plate or sheet of waxed paper. Put the olive oil and water in a pan and slowly bring to a boil. As soon as the water boils, remove the pan from the heat and quickly tip in the flour all at once. Using a wooden spoon, beat the mixture well until it is smooth and leaves the sides of the pan.

Let the mixture cool for 1–2 minutes, then add the eggs, beating hard after each addition and keeping the mixture stiff. Add the cheese and paprika, then season to taste with salt and pepper and mix well. Store the mixture in the refrigerator until you are ready to cook the cheese puffs.

Just before serving the cheese puffs, heat the corn oil in a deep fryer to 350–375°F/180–190°C, or until a cube of bread browns in 30 seconds. Drop teaspoonfuls of the prepared mixture, in batches, into the hot oil and cook for 2–3 minutes, turning once, or until golden brown and crispy. They should rise to the surface of the oil and puff up. Drain well on paper towels.

Serve the puffs piping hot, accompanied by the fiery salsa for dipping and toothpicks to spear the puffs.

cheese & olive
empanadillas

Since there are not many Spanish cheeses available outside Spain, you can choose to make these pastries with Manchego, Cheddar, Gruyère, Gouda, mozzarella, or a firm goat cheese. Large versions of these empanadillas are known as empanadas. *MAKES 26*

3 oz/85 g firm or soft cheese

generous ¹/₂ cup pitted green olives

¹/₃ cup sun-dried tomatoes in oil, drained

1³/₄ oz/50 g canned anchovy fillets, drained

pepper

2 oz/55 g sun-dried tomato paste

all-purpose flour, for dusting

1 lb 2 oz/500 g ready-made puff pastry, thawed if frozen

beaten egg, to glaze

Preheat the oven to 400°F/200°C. Cut the cheese into small dice measuring about ¹/₄ inch/5 mm. Chop the olives, sun-dried tomatoes, and anchovies into pieces about the same size as the cheese. Put all the chopped ingredients in a bowl and season with pepper to taste, then gently mix together. Stir in the sun-dried tomato paste.

On a lightly floured counter, thinly roll out the puff pastry. Using a plain, round 3¹/₄-inch/8-cm cutter, cut into 18 circles. Gently pile the trimmings together and roll out again, then cut out another 8 circles. Using a teaspoon, put a little of the prepared filling equally in the center of each of the pastry circles.

Dampen the edges of the pastry with a little water, then bring up the sides to cover the filling completely and pinch the edges together with your fingers to seal them. With the tip of a sharp knife, make a small slit in the top of each pastry. You can store the pastries in the refrigerator at this stage until you are ready to bake them.

Place the pastries on dampened baking sheets and brush each with a little beaten egg to glaze. Bake in the oven for 10–15 minutes, or until golden brown, crisp, and well risen. Serve the empanadillas piping hot, warm, or cold.

fried manchego cheese

Manchego is Spain's most famous cheese. It is sold at various stages of its maturity,
although the most widely available is the firm, full-flavored hard cheese,
as opposed to the soft, mild young cheese, which is rarely found outside Spain.

SERVES 6–8 AS PART OF A TAPAS MEAL

7 oz/200 g Manchego cheese

3 tbsp all-purpose flour

salt and pepper

1 egg

1 tsp water

1¹/₂ cups fresh white or brown bread crumbs

corn oil, for deep-frying

Slice the cheese into triangular shapes about ³/₄ inch/2 cm thick or alternatively into cubes measuring about the same size. Put the flour in a plastic bag and season with salt and pepper to taste. Break the egg into a shallow dish and beat together with the water. Spread the bread crumbs onto a plate.

Toss the cheese pieces in the flour so that they are evenly coated, then dip the cheese in the egg mixture. Finally, dip the cheese in the bread crumbs so that the pieces are coated on all sides. Transfer to a large plate and store in the refrigerator until you are ready to serve them.

Just before serving, heat about 1 inch/2.5 cm of the corn oil in a large, heavy-bottom skillet or heat the oil in a deep fryer to 350–375°F/180–190°C, or until a cube of bread browns in 30 seconds. Add the cheese, in batches of about 4 or 5 pieces so that the temperature of the oil does not drop, and cook for 1–2 minutes, turning once, until the cheese is just beginning to melt and the pieces are golden brown on all sides. Do make sure that the oil is hot enough; otherwise the coating on the cheese will take too long to become crisp and the cheese inside may ooze out.

Using a slotted spoon, remove the fried cheese from the skillet or deep fryer and drain well on paper towels. Serve the fried cheese pieces hot, accompanied by toothpicks on which to spear them.

variation

**Other cheeses work equally well here,
such as Cheddar, mozzarella, or even
a firm goat cheese.**

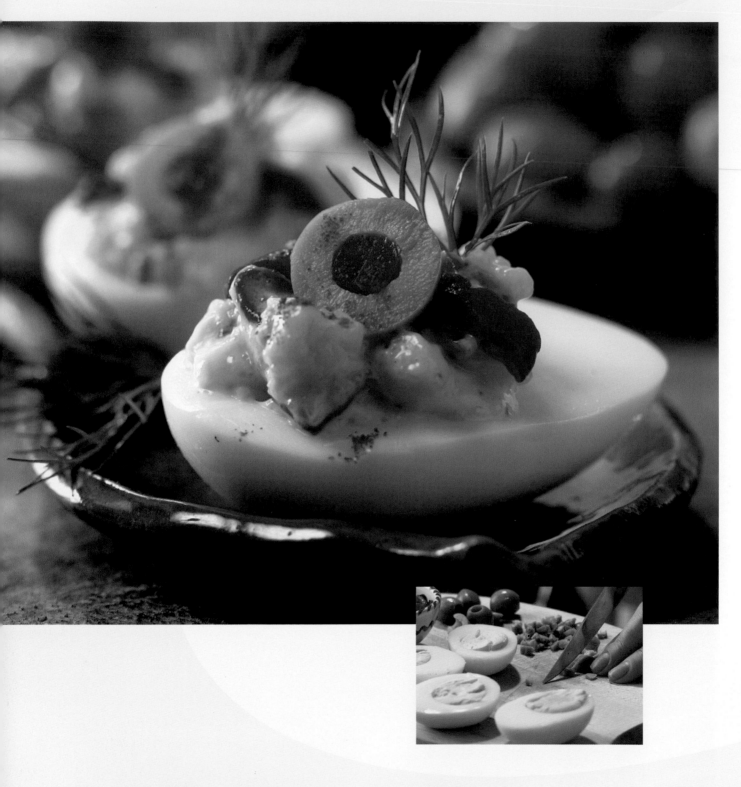

devilled eggs

In the south of Spain, the selection of dishes served in tapas bars would be considered incomplete without the inclusion of these Devilled Eggs and Tortilla Española (see page 70). As a variation, you could use rolled, canned anchovy fillets to garnish each egg. *MAKES 16*

8 large eggs

2 whole pimientos (sweet red bell peppers) from a jar or can

8 green olives

5 tbsp mayonnaise

8 drops Tabasco sauce

large pinch cayenne pepper

salt and pepper

paprika, for dusting

sprigs of fresh dill, to garnish

To cook the eggs, put them in a pan, then cover with cold water and slowly bring to a boil. Immediately reduce the heat to very low, then cover and simmer gently for 10 minutes. As soon as the eggs are cooked, drain them and put under cold running water until they are cold. By doing this quickly, it will prevent a black ring from forming around the egg yolk. Gently tap the eggs to crack the eggshells and let stand until cold. When cold, crack the shells all over and remove them.

Using a stainless steel knife, halve the eggs lengthwise, then carefully remove the yolks. Put the yolks in a nylon strainer, set over a bowl, and rub through, then mash them with a wooden spoon or fork. If necessary, rinse the egg whites under cold water and dry very carefully.

Put the pimientos on paper towels to dry well, then chop them finely, reserving a few strips.

Finely chop the olives. If you are going to pipe the filling into the eggs, you need to chop both these ingredients very finely so that they will go through a 1/2-inch/1-cm tip. Add the chopped pimientos and most of the chopped olives to the mashed egg yolks, reserving 16 larger pieces to garnish. Add the mayonnaise and mix well together, then add the Tabasco sauce, cayenne pepper, and salt and pepper to taste.

Finally put the egg yolk mixture into a pastry bag fitted with a 1/2-inch/1-cm plain tip and pipe the mixture into the hollow egg whites. Alternatively, for a simpler finish, use a teaspoon to spoon the prepared filling into each egg half.

Arrange the eggs on a serving plate. Add a small strip of the reserved pimientos and a piece of olive to the top of each stuffed egg. Dust with a little paprika and garnish with dill sprigs.

tortilla española

This is Spain's classic tapa (as well as the staple food for a picnic) and is made with potato, onion, and egg. Other ingredients can be added, such as ham, bacon, cheese, mushrooms, red or green bell peppers, asparagus, and artichoke hearts, but the Spanish prefer to keep it plain. *SERVES 8 AS PART OF A TAPAS MEAL*

1 lb/450 g waxy potatoes
generous 13/4 cups Spanish olive oil
2 onions, chopped

2 large eggs
salt and pepper
sprigs of fresh flatleaf parsley, to garnish

Peel the potatoes and cut into small cubes or wedges, then put on a clean dish towel and dry well. Heat the olive oil in a large, heavy-bottom or nonstick skillet. Add the potato pieces and onions, then reduce the heat and cook the potatoes, stirring frequently so that they do not clump together, for 20 minutes, or until they are tender but not browned. The secret of success is to cook the potatoes for a long time so that they absorb the flavor of the oil and are cooked but not browned or crisp, and do not fall apart. They are, in fact, almost boiled rather than fried.

Meanwhile, beat the eggs lightly in a large bowl and season well with salt and pepper. Place a strainer over a large bowl.

When the potatoes and onions are cooked, drain them into the strainer so that the bowl catches the oil. Reserve the oil for future use. When the potatoes and onions are well drained, gently stir them into the beaten eggs.

Wipe the skillet clean or wash it if necessary to prevent the tortilla from sticking. Heat 2 tablespoons of the reserved olive oil in the skillet. When hot, add the egg and potato mixture, then reduce the heat and cook for 3–5 minutes, or until the underside is just set. Use a spatula to push the potatoes down into the egg so that they are submerged, and keep loosening the tortilla from the bottom of the skillet to stop it sticking.

To cook the second side of the tortilla, cover it with a plate and hold the plate in place with the other hand. Drain off the oil in the skillet, then quickly turn the skillet upside down so that the tortilla falls onto the plate. Return the skillet to the heat and add a little more of the reserved oil to it if necessary. Slide the tortilla, cooked side uppermost, back into the pan and cook for an additional 3–5 minutes, or until set underneath. The tortilla is cooked when it is firm and crisp on the outside but still slightly runny in the center.

Slide the tortilla onto a serving plate and let stand for about 15 minutes. Serve it warm or cold, cut into small squares, fingers, or wedges and garnished with parsley sprigs.

fish & seafood

HERE there are eleven recipes that draw on a wide selection of fish and seafood. Included are recipes using cod, salmon, sardines, angler fish, tuna, crab, shrimp, calamares, scallops, and mussels.

cod & caper croquettes

The secret of cooking croquettes successfully is to chill the mixture in the refrigerator before cooking. You will then find they do not disintegrate when put in the hot oil. As a matter of interest, Spain is the world's largest producer of capers! *MAKES 12*

12 oz/350 g white fish fillets, such as cod, haddock or angler fish

1¹/4 cups milk

salt and pepper

4 tbsp olive oil or ¹/2 stick butter

¹/3 cup all-purpose flour

4 tbsp capers, coarsely chopped

1 tsp paprika

1 garlic clove, crushed

1 tsp lemon juice

3 tbsp chopped fresh flatleaf parsley, plus extra sprigs to garnish

1 egg, beaten

1 cup fresh white bread crumbs

1 tbsp sesame seeds

corn oil, for deep-frying

lemon wedges, to garnish

mayonnaise, to serve

Put the fish fillets in a large, heavy-bottom skillet. Pour in the milk and season to taste with salt and pepper. Bring to a boil, then reduce the heat and simmer gently, covered, for 8–10 minutes, or until the fish flakes easily when tested with a fork. Using a spatula, remove the fish from the skillet. Pour the milk into a pitcher and reserve. Flake the fish, removing and discarding the skin and bones.

Heat the olive oil in a pan. Stir in the flour to form a paste and cook gently, stirring, for 1 minute. Remove the pan from the heat and gradually stir in the reserved milk until smooth. Return to the heat and bring to a boil, stirring all the time, until the mixture thickens.

Remove the pan from the heat, then add the flaked fish and beat until the mixture is smooth. Add the capers, paprika, garlic, lemon juice, and parsley and mix well. Season the mixture to taste with salt and pepper. Spread the fish mixture in a dish and let cool, then cover and put in the refrigerator for 2–3 hours or overnight.

When the fish mixture has chilled, pour the beaten egg onto a plate. Put the bread crumbs and sesame seeds on a separate plate and mix together, then spread out. Divide the fish mixture into 12 equal-size portions. With lightly floured hands, form each portion into a sausage shape, measuring about 3 inches/7.5 cm in length. Dip the croquettes, one at a time, in the beaten egg, then roll in the bread crumb mixture to coat them. Place on a plate and chill in the refrigerator for about 1 hour.

To cook the croquettes, heat the oil in a deep fryer to 350–375°F/180–190°C. Add the croquettes, in batches, and cook for 3 minutes. Remove from the pan with a slotted spoon and drain them well on paper towels.

Serve piping hot, garnished with lemon wedges and parsley sprigs and accompanied by a bowl of mayonnaise for dipping.

fresh salmon
in mojo sauce

Mojo sauce is also known as Canary Island Red Sauce, after its place of origin.
When served without the paprika but with finely chopped fresh cilantro and parsley leaves,
it is known as Canary Island Green Sauce. It is also good drizzled over boiled new potatoes.

SERVES 8 AS PART OF A TAPAS MEAL

**4 fresh salmon fillets, weighing
about 1 lb 10 oz/750 g in total
salt and pepper
3 tbsp Spanish olive oil
1 fresh flatleaf parsley sprig, to garnish**

Mojo Sauce
**2 garlic cloves, peeled
2 tsp paprika
1 tsp ground cumin
5 tbsp Spanish extra virgin olive oil
2 tbsp white wine vinegar
salt**

To prepare the mojo sauce, put the garlic, paprika, and cumin in the bowl of a food processor fitted with the metal blade and, using a pulsing action, blend for 1 minute to mix well together. With the motor still running, add 1 tablespoon of the olive oil, drop by drop, through the feeder tube. When it has been added, scrape down the sides of the bowl with a spatula, then very slowly continue to pour in the oil in a thin, steady stream, until all the oil has been added and the sauce has slightly thickened. Add the vinegar and blend for an additional 1 minute. Season with salt to taste.

To prepare the salmon, remove the skin and cut each fillet in half widthwise, then cut lengthwise into 3/4-inch/2-cm thick slices, discarding any bones. Season the pieces of fish to taste with salt and pepper.

Heat the olive oil in a large, heavy-bottom skillet. When hot, add the pieces of fish and cook for about 10 minutes, depending on its thickness, turning occasionally until cooked and browned on both sides.

Transfer the salmon to a warmed serving dish. Drizzle over some of the sauce and serve hot, garnished with parsley and accompanied by the remaining sauce in a small serving bowl.

sardines marinated in sherry vinegar

Sherry vinegar is ideal for marinating fish such as sardines, trout, or salmon.

SERVES 6 AS PART OF A TAPAS MEAL

12 small fresh sardines
3/4 cup Spanish olive oil
4 tbsp sherry vinegar
2 carrots, cut into julienne strips
1 onion, thinly sliced
1 garlic clove, crushed
1 bay leaf
salt and pepper
4 tbsp chopped fresh flatleaf parsley
few sprigs of fresh dill, to garnish
lemon wedges, to serve

If it has not already been done, clean the fish by scraping the scales off with a knife, being careful not to cut the skin. The choice is yours whether you then leave the heads and tails on or cut them off and discard. Slit along the belly of each fish and remove the innards under cold running water. Then dry each fish well on paper towels.

Heat 4 tablespoons of the olive oil in a large, heavy-bottom skillet. Add the sardines and cook for 10 minutes, or until browned on both sides. Using a spatula, very carefully remove the sardines from the skillet and transfer to a large, shallow, nonmetallic dish that will hold the sardines in a single layer.

Gently heat the remaining olive oil and the sherry vinegar in a large pan, then add the carrot strips, onion, garlic, and bay leaf and simmer gently for 5 minutes, or until softened. Season the vegetables to taste with salt and pepper. Let the mixture cool slightly, then pour the marinade over the sardines.

Cover the dish and let the sardines cool before transferring to the refrigerator. Let marinate for about 8 hours or overnight, spooning the marinade over the sardines occasionally, although there is no need to get up in the night! Return the sardines to room temperature before serving, then sprinkle with parsley and garnish with dill sprigs. Serve with lemon wedges.

variation

Fresh trout or salmon fillets can be used, but
instead of cooking the fish, it is better to
steam the fillets for 5 minutes. When cooked,
slice each fillet in half lengthwise. You will
need 6 fish fillets in total for this recipe.

angler fish, rosemary
& bacon skewers

Angler fish, also known as monkfish, is ideal for skewers because of its firm texture, but other firm-fleshed fish, such as cod, swordfish, or tuna, would make ideal alternatives. Instead of using rosemary stems, you can use the more traditional metal skewers or wooden bamboo skewers. The latter should be presoaked in cold water for 30 minutes to prevent them from burning. *MAKES 12*

12 oz/350 g angler fish fillet

12 stems of fresh rosemary

3 tbsp Spanish olive oil

juice of 1/2 small lemon

1 garlic clove, crushed

salt and pepper

6 thick strips Canadian bacon

lemon wedges, to garnish

Aïoli (see page 53), to serve

If using whole angler fish tail, cut either side of the central bone with a sharp knife and remove the flesh to form 2 fillets. Slice the fillets in half lengthwise, then cut each fillet into 12 bite-size chunks to give a total of 24 pieces. Put the angler fish pieces in a large bowl.

To prepare the rosemary skewers, strip the leaves off the stems and reserve them, leaving a few leaves at one end.

For the marinade, finely chop the reserved leaves and whisk together in a bowl with the olive oil, lemon juice, garlic, and salt and pepper to taste. Add the angler fish pieces and toss until coated in the marinade. Cover and let marinate in the refrigerator for 1–2 hours.

Cut each bacon strip in half lengthwise, then in half widthwise, and roll up each piece. Thread 2 pieces of angler fish alternately with 2 bacon rolls onto the prepared rosemary skewers.

Preheat the broiler, grill pan, or grill. If you are cooking the skewers under an overhead broiler, arrange them on the broiler pan so that the leaves of the rosemary skewers protrude from the broiler and therefore do not catch fire during cooking. Broil the angler fish and bacon skewers for 10 minutes, turning from time to time and basting with any remaining marinade, or until cooked. Serve hot, garnished with lemon wedges for squeezing over them and accompanied by a bowl of aïoli in which to dip the angler fish skewers.

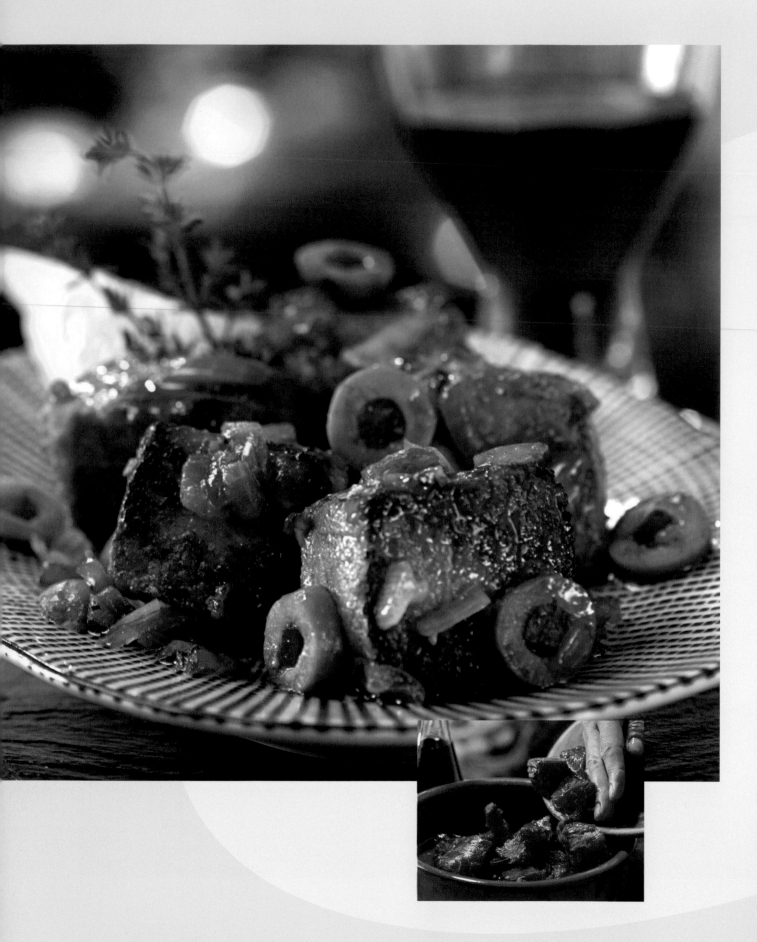

tuna with
pimiento-stuffed olives

Now that tuna can easily be bought fresh, it is a real treat. It has a firm flesh and a superb flavor. Once cooked—broiled, fried, baked, or braised—you can eat it as a steak or exactly the same way as you would canned tuna. *SERVES 6 AS PART OF A TAPAS MEAL*

2 fresh tuna steaks, weighing about 9 oz/
250 g in total and about 1 inch/2.5 cm thick

5 tbsp Spanish olive oil

3 tbsp red wine vinegar

4 sprigs of fresh thyme, plus extra to garnish

1 bay leaf

salt and pepper

2 tbsp all-purpose flour

1 onion, finely chopped

2 garlic cloves, finely chopped

scant 2/3 cup pimiento-stuffed green olives,
sliced

crusty bread, to serve

The tuna steaks need to be marinated, so do remember to start preparing the dish the day before you are going to serve it. Remove the skin from the tuna steaks, then cut the steaks in half along the grain of the fish. Cut each half into 1/2-inch/1-cm thick slices against the grain.

Put 3 tablespoons of the olive oil and the vinegar in a large, shallow, nonmetallic dish.

Strip the leaves from the sprigs of thyme and add these to the dish with the bay leaf and salt and pepper to taste. Add the prepared strips of tuna, then cover the dish and let marinate in the refrigerator for 8 hours or overnight.

The next day, put the flour in a plastic bag. Remove the tuna strips from the marinade, reserving the marinade for later, then add them to the bag of flour and toss well until they are lightly coated.

Heat the remaining olive oil in a large, heavy-bottom skillet. Add the onion and garlic and gently cook for 5–10 minutes, or until softened and golden brown. Add the tuna strips to the skillet and cook for 2–5 minutes, turning several times, until the fish becomes opaque. Add the reserved marinade and olives to the skillet and cook for an additional 1–2 minutes, stirring, until the fish is tender and the sauce has thickened.

Serve the tuna and olives piping hot, garnished with thyme sprigs. Accompany with slices of crusty bread for mopping up the sauce.

crab tartlets

You only have to look along the shelves of a Spanish supermarket to see the numerous varieties of canned fish that are available. On that note, canned salmon or tuna could easily be used in this recipe in place of the crabmeat. *MAKES 24*

1 tbsp Spanish olive oil

1 small onion, finely chopped

1 garlic clove, finely chopped

splash of dry white wine

2 eggs

^{2}/$_3$ cup milk or light cream

6 oz/175 g canned crabmeat, drained

2 oz/55 g Manchego or Parmesan cheese, grated

2 tbsp chopped fresh flatleaf parsley

pinch of freshly grated nutmeg

salt and pepper

sprigs of fresh dill, to garnish

Pastry

2^1/$_3$ cups all-purpose flour, plus extra for dusting

pinch of salt

1^1/$_2$ sticks butter

2 tbsp cold water

OR

1 lb 2 oz/500 g ready-made unsweetened pastry

Preheat the oven to 375°F/190°C. To prepare the crabmeat filling, heat the olive oil in a pan, then add the onion and cook for 5 minutes, or until softened but not browned. Add the garlic and cook for an additional 30 seconds. Add a splash of wine and cook for 1–2 minutes, or until most of the wine has evaporated.

Lightly whisk the eggs in a large mixing bowl, then whisk in the milk or cream. Add the crabmeat, cheese, parsley, and the onion mixture. Season the mixture with nutmeg and salt and pepper to taste and mix well together.

To prepare the pastry if you are making it yourself, mix the flour and salt together in a large mixing bowl. Add the butter, cut into small pieces, and rub in until the mixture resembles fine bread crumbs. Gradually stir in enough of the water to form a firm dough. Alternatively, the pastry could be made in a food processor.

On a lightly floured counter, thinly roll out the pastry. Using a plain, round 2^3/$_4$-inch/7-cm cutter, cut the pastry into 18 circles. Gently pile the trimmings together and roll out again, then cut out an additional 6 circles. Use to line 24 x 1^1/$_2$-inch/4-cm tartlet pans.

Carefully spoon the crabmeat mixture into the pastry shells, taking care not to overfill them.

Bake the tartlets in the oven for 25–30 minutes until browned and set. Then serve the crab tartlets hot or cold, garnished with fresh dill sprigs.

lime-drizzled shrimp

This dish can also be prepared with cooked fresh or frozen shrimp. Make sure that you dry them very well on paper towels before using and, as they are already cooked, add them to the skillet for just 1–2 minutes, simply to heat them through.

SERVES 6 AS PART OF A TAPAS MEAL

4 limes	splash of dry sherry
12 raw jumbo shrimp, in their shells	salt and pepper
3 tbsp Spanish olive oil	4 tbsp chopped fresh
2 garlic cloves, finely chopped	flatleaf parsley

Grate the rind and squeeze out the juice from 2 of the limes. Cut the remaining 2 limes into wedges and reserve for later.

To prepare the shrimp, remove the legs, leaving the shells and tails intact. Using a sharp knife, make a shallow slit along the top of each

shrimp, then pull out the dark vein and discard. Rinse the shrimp under cold water and dry well on paper towels.

Heat the olive oil in a large, heavy-bottom skillet. Add the garlic and cook for 30 seconds. Add the shrimp and cook for 5 minutes, stirring from time to time, or until they turn pink and begin to curl. Mix in the lime rind, juice, and a splash of sherry to moisten, then stir well.

Transfer the cooked shrimp to a serving dish, then season to taste with salt and pepper and sprinkle over the parsley. Serve piping hot, accompanied by the reserved lime wedges for squeezing over the shrimp.

sizzling chili shrimp

The point of this dish is that the pan is brought to the table and the shrimp are served really hot, hence their name. The oil should still be sizzling, so it is usually served with a plate of bread perched on top.

SERVES 8 AS PART OF A TAPAS MEAL

To prepare the shrimp, pull off their heads. With your fingers, peel off their shells, leaving the tails intact. Using a sharp knife, make a shallow slit along the top of each shrimp, then pull out the dark vein and discard. Rinse the shrimp under cold water and dry well on paper towels.

Cut the chili in half lengthwise, remove the seeds and finely chop the flesh. It is important either to wear gloves or to wash your hands very thoroughly after chopping chilies, as their juices can cause irritation to sensitive skin, especially around the eyes, nose, or mouth. Whatever you do, do not rub your eyes after touching the cut flesh of the chili.

Heat the olive oil in a large, heavy-bottom skillet or flameproof casserole until quite hot, then add the garlic and cook for 30 seconds. Add the shrimp, chili, paprika, and a pinch of salt and cook for 2–3 minutes, stirring all the time, until the shrimp turn pink and begin to curl.

Serve the shrimp in the cooking dish, still sizzling. Accompany with toothpicks, to spear the shrimp, and chunks or slices of crusty bread to mop up the aromatic cooking oil.

1 lb 2 oz/500 g raw jumbo shrimp, in their shells
1 small fresh red chili
6 tbsp Spanish olive oil
2 garlic cloves, finely chopped
pinch of paprika
salt
crusty bread, to serve

calamares

Squid is available already prepared and sliced into rings, but if you have the time it is better to prepare it yourself. *SERVES 6 AS PART OF A TAPAS MEAL*

1 lb/450 g prepared squid (see cook's tip)
all-purpose flour, for coating
corn oil, for deep-frying

salt
lemon wedges, to garnish
Aïoli (see page 53), to serve

Slice the squid into 1/2-inch/1-cm rings and halve the tentacles if large. Rinse and dry well on paper towels so that they do not spit during cooking. Dust the squid pieces with flour so that they are lightly coated. Do not season the flour, as Spanish cooks will tell you that seasoning squid with salt before cooking toughens it. They should know!

Heat the corn oil in a deep fryer to 350–375°F/180–190°C, or until a cube of bread browns in 30 seconds. Carefully add the squid pieces, in batches so that the temperature of the oil does not drop, and cook for 2–3 minutes, or until golden brown and crisp all over, turning several times. Do not overcook, or the squid will become tough and rubbery rather than moist and tender.

Using a slotted spoon, remove the fried squid from the deep fryer and drain well on paper towels. Keep warm in the oven while you cook the remaining squid pieces.

Sprinkle the fried squid with salt and serve piping hot, garnished with lemon wedges for squeezing over them. Accompany with a bowl of aïoli in which to dip the calamares.

cook's tip

If you need to prepare the squid yourself, hold the body in one hand and pull on the head and tentacles with the other. The body contents will come away too and can be discarded. Cut off the edible tentacles just above the eyes and discard the head. Remove the ink sacs from the head carefully so that you do not pierce them. Remove the backbone and peel off the thin, dark outer skin.

scallops in saffron sauce

Shelled scallops are available, both fresh and frozen, from supermarkets and fish dealers. Should you buy them from a fish dealer, ask if you can have some shells, as they make attractive serving dishes. You will need to scrub them clean before use.

SERVES 8 AS PART OF A TAPAS MEAL

²/₃ cup dry white wine

²/₃ cup fish stock

large pinch of saffron strands

2 lb/900 g shelled scallops, preferably large ones

salt and pepper

3 tbsp Spanish olive oil

1 small onion, finely chopped

2 garlic cloves, finely chopped

²/₃ cup heavy cream

squeeze of lemon juice

chopped fresh flatleaf parsley, to garnish

crusty bread, to serve

Put the wine, fish stock, and saffron in a pan and bring to a boil. Reduce the heat, then cover and simmer gently for 15 minutes.

Meanwhile, remove and discard from each scallop the tough, white muscle that is found opposite the coral, and separate the coral from the scallop. Slice the scallops vertically into thick slices, including the corals if they are present. Dry the scallops well on paper towels, then season to taste with salt and pepper.

Heat the olive oil in a large, heavy-bottom skillet. Add the onion and garlic and cook for 5 minutes, or until softened and lightly browned. Add the sliced scallops to the pan and cook gently for 5 minutes, stirring occasionally, or until they just turn opaque. The secret is not to overcook the scallops, or they will become tough and rubbery.

Using a slotted spoon, remove the scallops from the skillet and transfer to a warmed plate. Add the saffron liquid to the skillet and bring to a boil, then boil rapidly until reduced to about half. Reduce the heat and gradually stir in the cream, just a little at a time. Simmer gently until the sauce thickens.

Return the scallops to the skillet and simmer for 1–2 minutes just to heat them through. Add a squeeze of lemon juice and season to taste with salt and pepper. Serve the scallops hot, garnished with the parsley and accompanied by chunks or slices of crusty bread to mop up the saffron sauce.

mussels with
herb & garlic butter

Due to the lack of lush pastureland in most of Spain, dairy cattle are not
extensively raised and therefore oil, as opposed to butter, is more commonly used in cooking.
Nevertheless, butter is occasionally used, as illustrated in this recipe.

SERVES 8 AS PART OF A TAPAS MEAL

1 lb 12 oz/800 g fresh mussels, in their shells

splash of dry white wine

1 bay leaf

3/4 stick butter

generous 1/2 cup fresh bread crumbs

4 tbsp chopped fresh flatleaf parsley,
plus extra sprigs to garnish

2 tbsp snipped fresh chives

2 garlic cloves, finely chopped

salt and pepper

lemon wedges, to serve

Clean the mussels by scrubbing or scraping the shells and pulling out any beards that are attached to them. Discard any with broken shells and any that refuse to close when tapped. Put the mussels in a colander and rinse well under cold running water. Preheat the oven to 450°F/230°C.

Put the mussels in a large pan and add a splash of wine and the bay leaf. Cook, covered, over high heat for 5 minutes, shaking the pan occasionally, or until the mussels are opened. Drain the mussels and discard any that remain closed.

Shell the mussels, reserving one half of each shell. Arrange the mussels, in their half-shells, in a large, shallow, ovenproof serving dish.

Melt the butter and pour into a small bowl. Add the bread crumbs, parsley, chives, garlic, and salt and pepper to taste and mix well together. Let stand until the butter has set slightly. Using your fingers or 2 teaspoons, take a large pinch of the herb and butter mixture and use to fill each mussel shell, pressing it down well. Chill the filled mussels in the refrigerator until ready to serve.

To serve, bake the mussels in the oven for 10 minutes, or until hot. Serve immediately, garnished with parsley sprigs and accompanied by lemon wedges for squeezing over them.

index